W9-AUI-657

DINOSAUR

LONDON, NEW YORK,
MELBOURNE, MUNICH, AND DELHI

Senior Editor   Niki Foreman
Senior Art Editor   Philip Letsu
Editor   Steven Carton
Designers   Johnny Pau, Jane Thomas

Managing Editor   Linda Esposito
Managing Art Editor   Jim Green

Category Publisher   Laura Buller
Design Development Manager   Sophia M Tampakopoulos

Production Controller   Charlotte Oliver
Production Editor   Marc Staples
DK Picture Library   Emma Shepherd
Picture Research   Ria Jones
Additional Picture Research   Frances Vargo
Jacket Editor   Matilda Gollon
Jacket Designer   Natalie Godwin

3-D Digital Sculptor   Peter Minister
3-D Digital Enhancer   Arran Lewis

For Digital Labs International:
Director   Maurice Linscott
Director of Animation   Rob Cook
Programmer   Steve Clare

AUGMENTED BY
TOTAL IMMERSION

First published in Great Britain in 2011
by Dorling Kindersley Limited,
80 Strand, London WC2R 0RL

A Penguin Company

Copyright © 2011 Dorling Kindersley Limited

2 4 6 8 10 9 7 5 3 1
179065 – 13/12/2010

All rights reserved. No part of this publication may be
reproduced, stored in a retrieval system, or transmitted
in any form or by any means, electronic,
mechanical, photocopying, recording,
or otherwise, without the prior written
permission of the copyright owner.

A CIP catalogue record for this book
is available from the British Library.

ISBN 978-1-40536-303-7

Hi-res workflow
proofed by MDP, UK

Printed and bound
in China by Toppan

Discover more at
www.dk.com

PRIMARY LIBRARY
ST STEPHEN'S SCHOOL
1379

PN
567
.9
WOO

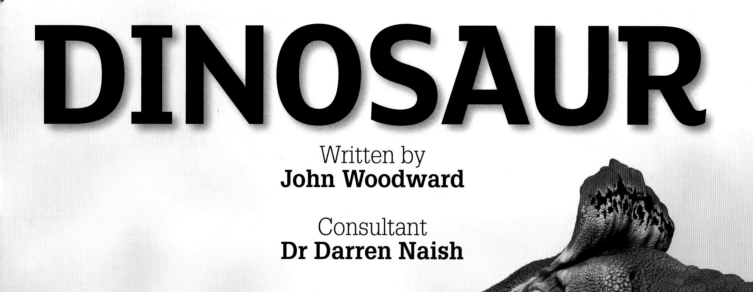

DINOSAUR

Written by
John Woodward

Consultant
Dr Darren Naish

Contents

HOW TO INSTALL THE SOFTWARE

1 Download the software from www.3Dpops.dkonline.com and follow the on-screen instructions to install the software on your computer.

2 In the book there are six Augmented Reality (AR) spreads. Look for the blue logo in the right-hand corner of the page.

Show the main image to your webcam to start the AR animation.

3 Sit in front of the computer with the book in front of you and your webcam turned on, and ensure that your book is in view of the webcam.

Tyranno

CRIPPLING BITE

FAVOURED PREY

:tack

The most powerful land predator that ever lived. Tyrannosaurus rex was massively built with immensely strong jaws and teeth. These equipped it for a uniquely devastating attack technique – charging straight in and biting huge chunks out of its living victims.

AGILE STANCE

POWERFUL LEGS

HUGE SKULL

AR logo is in the right-hand corner of the AR spread.

Place your hand over each trigger box in turn to control the dinosaurs' actions.

4 Show the central image on the open page to the webcam and the AR animation will jump to life from the pages of your book and appear on your computer screen.

5 To see the next part of the animation and make the dinosaurs do different things, place your hand over one of the trigger boxes. Each trigger box is labelled with a hand symbol to show that it is a trigger box, and the boxes are numbered in the order that they should be covered.

Minimum system requirements

Windows PC
Windows XP with DirectX 9.0c
(or Windows XP SP2), Windows Vista Intel P4
2.4 GHz or Amd equivalent
1 Gb RAM
Supports most graphics cards (Nvidia, ATI, Chipset Intel) except Via chipset

Macintosh
Mac OS 10.4, 10.5, 10.6
Intel Dual Core (or Core 2 duo) 2.4Ghz
1 Gb RAM
Supports graphics cards Nvidia, ATI
(Macs based on Power PC processor are not supported)

Dinosaur science

The dinosaurs are the most spectacularly successful animals that have ever lived. They dominated life on Earth for 165 million years, and one branch of the dinosaur line still survives today as the birds. Huge advances in dinosaur science have been made over the past few decades – in fact, at least 80 per cent of all known dinosaurs have been named since 1990. These new discoveries have been matched by some of the most exciting research ever attempted.

Fossil *Microraptor* – a feathered dinosaur

The Mesozoic world

The great age of the dinosaurs began about 230 million years ago in the Mesozoic – an era of Earth's history that lasted for 186 million years. At the end of the Mesozoic most of the dinosaurs were wiped out in a catastrophic extinction. But some survived and still live all around us today – the birds.

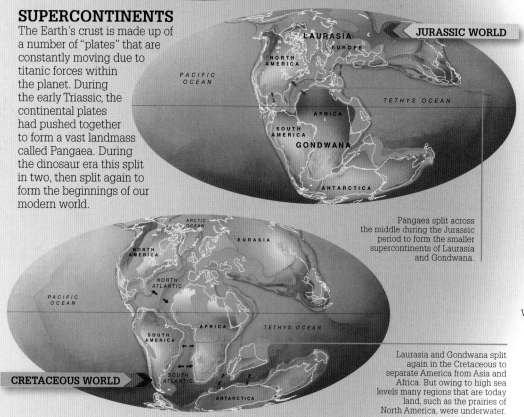

TRIASSIC WORLD

The heart of Pangaea was arid desert, but during the Triassic the Tethys Ocean opened up between the northern and southern parts of the supercontinent, making the climate less hostile.

JURASSIC WORLD

Pangaea split across the middle during the Jurassic period to form the smaller supercontinents of Laurasia and Gondwana.

CRETACEOUS WORLD

Laurasia and Gondwana split again in the Cretaceous to separate America from Asia and Africa. But owing to high sea levels many regions that are today land, such as the prairies of North America, were underwater.

SUPERCONTINENTS

The Earth's crust is made up of a number of "plates" that are constantly moving due to titanic forces within the planet. During the early Triassic, the continental plates had pushed together to form a vast landmass called Pangaea. During the dinosaur era this split in two, then split again to form the beginnings of our modern world.

DEEP TIME

The Mesozoic consisted of the Triassic, Jurassic, and Cretaceous periods. Many of the most famous dinosaurs lived in the later Cretaceous, which is named after the chalk rock that formed at this time in warm tropical seas. The rock is composed of the remains of trillions of microscopic organisms that collected – at the same rate that dust settles – on the sea floor. The rock's immense depth of up to 400 m (1,300 ft) shows the vast span of time occupied by just part of the Mesozoic era.

WARMER WORLD

During the Mesozoic the global climate was warmer than it is today. Many regions that now support tropical rainforests were deserts in the Triassic, and trees grew on Antarctica in the Jurassic. But some areas had cold winters, especially in the Cretaceous, and dinosaurs lived in both the warm and cold zones.

ERA	MESOZOIC ERA		
PERIOD	Triassic	Jurassic	
MILLIONS OF YEARS AGO	251	199	145

PLANT LIFE

At the start of the dinosaur age there were no flowering plants, so plant-eating dinosaurs fed on clubmosses, horsetails, and ferns, or gathered the foliage of conifer, cycad, and ginkgo trees. These plants grew very lushly in the warm Mesozoic climate, creating plenty of food. Flowering plants appeared in the Cretaceous period, providing dinosaurs with new types of food such as fruit.

The two tusks of the hippo-sized *Placerias* were probably social display features, but its beaked jaws were ideal for gathering leafy plants.

ANIMAL LIFE

When dinosaurs first appeared, the dominant animals were larger reptiles such as crurotarsans – the group that includes crocodiles. There were also amphibians, mammal ancestors such as this *Placerias*, tortoises, lizards, marine reptiles, pterosaurs, and small invertebrates such as insects and spiders. However, an extinction at the end of the Triassic eliminated most of the dinosaurs' competitors, allowing the dinosaurs to take over.

➤➤ END OF AN ERA

Roughly 65 million years ago the Mesozoic era ended in a mass extinction, probably caused by an asteroid striking what is now the Yucatán in Mexico. Most dinosaurs were eliminated, along with the pterosaurs, marine reptiles, and other animals like these ammonites – but birds and mammals survived.

➤➤ TIMELINE

The dinosaurs appeared halfway through the Triassic and flourished for 165 million years until the end of the Mesozoic. The Cenozoic – our own era – has lasted less than half as long, showing the dinosaurs to be some of the most successful animals that have ever lived.

CENOZOIC ERA		
Cretaceous	Paleogene	Neogene
65	23	0

Dinosaurs defined

The dinosaurs are part of a group of reptiles called the archosaurs, which also includes the pterosaurs, crocodilians, and birds (which are avian dinosaurs). From the tiny, feathered sparrows of today to the giant, scaly tyrannosaurids of the Cretaceous, the archosaurs encompass a diverse array of animals, all of which are distinguished by a large cavity on the side of their skulls.

The large cavity on each side of the skull between the nostril and eye socket is a feature of all archosaurs.

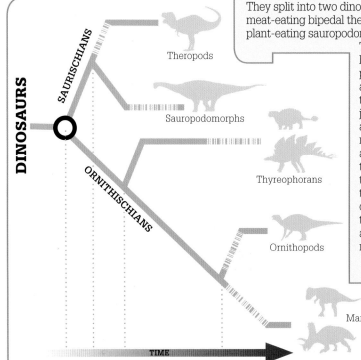

HIGH WALK

All dinosaurs share some distinctive skeletal features that show they walked with their legs upright beneath their bodies instead of sprawling like lizards. Their bones also show clear evidence of powerful muscles that were capable of supporting the animals' weight. Many, like this *Tyrannosaurus*, walked on their long hind legs like modern birds. The erect gait of the dinosaurs is one of their most distinctive features.

ORIGINS

Dinosaur-like archosaurs had evolved by the start of the mid-Triassic, 10 million years earlier than the oldest known true dinosaurs. These early archosaurs included *Asilisaurus*, whose remains were discovered in southern Tanzania in 2008. Although quite small by dinosaur standards, it had long, slender limbs and an erect walk, much like the dinosaurs' direct ancestors.

FAMILY TREE

Early in their history dinosaurs divided into two groups – the saurischians and ornithischians. Saurischians had longer necks, and most had forward-pointing pubis bones in the pelvis. They split into two dinosaur types: the largely meat-eating bipedal theropods, and the mainly plant-eating sauropodomorphs.

The ornithischians had backward-pointing pubis bones and a predentary bone at the tip of the lower jaw that supported a beak. They were mostly plant-eaters, and diversified into the armour-plated thyreophorans, the mainly bipedal ornithopods, and the horned and boneheaded marginocephalians.

DINOSAURS

SAURISCHIANS

ORNITHISCHIANS

Theropods

Sauropodomorphs

Thyreophorans

Ornithopods

Marginocephalians

TIME

AMAZING DIVERSITY

We usually think of dinosaurs as bloodthirsty hunters, colossal long-necked sauropods, or lumbering heavyweights armoured with plates and spikes. But many dinosaurs were quite small, and a few could even sit in the palm of your hand. Some, like this *Caudipteryx*, had feathers and were probably very colourful. Several had beaks rather than teeth, and many had spectacular display crests of bone and horn.

One group of archosaurs took to the air to become the pterosaurs, which were closely related to the dinosaurs. They had rather bat-like wings made of skin, and their bodies were covered with a form of fur. Unlike dinosaurs, they all became extinct at the end of the Mesozoic era.

The thigh bone of a dinosaur had a fully inturned head, much like that of a human but more loose-fitting. The hip joint was therefore lined with cartilage to support the head of the femur, and enabled the dinosaurs to move easily – essential for such active animals.

Long, heavy tails were held extended by those dinosaurs that stood on their back legs, to balance their bodies at the hips.

MARINE REPTILES

The marine counterparts of dinosaurs were only distant relatives, and not even archosaurs. Some early forms hunted at sea but probably bred on land, like seals. More familiar types such as this *Ichthyosaurus* and the long-necked plesiosaurs were fully oceanic, like whales, and a few were among the most powerful predators that ever lived. They all died out at the end of the Mesozoic.

The forearms of saurischians such as *Tyrannosaurus* were less mobile than ours, but were strong and effective for grabbing and holding prey.

Scientists have now named more than 800 species of dinosaurs.

Hinge-like ankle joints were a feature of all dinosaurs and indicate that they walked with their legs erect.

Three functional toes on each foot and a smaller toe on the inside were a feature of most theropods.

Fossil evidence

Everything that we know about extinct dinosaurs is derived from fossils – the remains or traces of dead organisms that have survived the decay process following death. Scientists can use these fossils to work out what a dinosaur looked like, and even how it lived.

OLD BONES

Most dinosaur fossils are of bones and teeth – the hardest parts of the body – which were buried in mud or sand that later turned to rock. Minerals in the rock then seeped into the remains, turning the bones to stone. Sometimes the bones remain joined together, as with this *Barosaurus* skeleton, but usually they are scattered, and in many cases only a few survive. But in regions where conditions did not favour fossilization there must be many dinosaurs that are lost forever.

Features like the amazingly long neck of *Barosaurus* are easy to deduce from fossils, especially if all the bones are articulated – that is, linked together as a skeleton.

The stomach contents of the dinosaur are preserved in some fossils, enabling us to see what it was eating when it died. Scientists have even found dinosaur coprolites – fossilized dung!

FOSSIL FOOD

Fossils also preserve evidence of the dinosaurs' world. This fossil fern is one of many fossilized plants that have survived from the Jurassic period, when *Barosaurus* was alive. They show that the vegetation was dominated by primitive plants such as ferns, conifers, and cycads. These still grow today, so we know exactly what type of plant this giant herbivore was eating.

The Zucheng fossil site in China has yielded more than 7,000 dinosaur bones.

Jaws and skulls are the most informative parts of any fossil skeleton. They give clues to the animal's diet, senses, and even its intelligence.

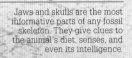

Tail bones often survive, but give little clue about how the tail was held. We once thought it was trailed on the ground, but scientists now think that it was held high.

The ridge of horny spines shown along the back of this dinosaur has not fossilized. But scientists think it was likely to have been present because similar dinosaurs had them.

SKIN

1 Soft tissue such as skin usually decays before it can be fossilized. But skin impressions like this one are sometimes found in fossilized mud. Other fossils preserve feathers, spines, and even traces of muscles. These rare remains help us to reconstruct how the animals looked in life.

Clothe the skeleton with skin

Big, thick bones like this thigh bone are the most likely to survive as fossils. But just one bone like this can be enough to identify a new species of dinosaur.

TEETH

2 Teeth fossilize well. This is very useful, because scientists can tell a lot about an animal from its teeth. These blunt, peg-shaped teeth were typical of some big plant-eating sauropods like *Barosaurus*, which would have used them to strip leaves from trees.

Make *Barosaurus* walk and then eat

Some fossils look very much like the bones of living animals. Those of *Barosaurus's* hind feet are like the bones of elephant feet, so we can guess that they looked similar in life, too.

Tracing the past

Recovering dinosaur fossils is a job for experts who know how to clean, conserve, and identify them. They can then use modern techniques to analyse their structure, work out how they fitted together, and put flesh back on the bones to reconstruct the appearance of the living animal.

As these dinosaur bones are exposed from a site in northeast China, their relative positions are recorded and each one is labelled. This will help the scientists to work out how the bones fit together.

RECOVERY

Although some fossilized dinosaur bones look massive, they are surprisingly fragile and must be excavated very carefully. First the scientists record their precise location and check the site for other dinosaur clues, such as traces of soft tissue, food, nests, eggs and young, and possible causes of death. Then they chip away the overlying rock to expose the fossils, reinforcing large bones with plaster before undercutting and removing them.

CONSERVATION

When a fossil arrives in the laboratory it is usually still partly encased in rock, as well as its protective plaster jacket. Skilled workers strip away the plaster and carefully remove as much of the rock as necessary. They also repair damaged specimens with special glues and other materials. It is slow, exacting work. Here, the skull of the *Tyrannosaurus rex* "Sue" is being cleaned up, shortly after its discovery in 1990.

IDENTIFICATION

Normally the scientists who excavate a fossil bone have a good idea about what it is. But if there is something novel about it, a full description will be published so that other scientists can read about it. At this point, a "new" dinosaur gets given a name. Some fossils defy identification, however. This 2.4-m- (8-ft-) brachiosaur shoulder bone was found in 1979, but has still not been linked to a named dinosaur.

FILLING THE GAPS

Complete skeletons are very rare. Most fossils are scattered bones, bone fragments, or even just a few teeth. But the missing bits of many broken bones can be restored by comparing them with the complete bones of similar animals – both modern and prehistoric. And if a few of the scattered bones have the same basic form as those of related dinosaurs, then scientists can confidently identify and reconstruct the whole creature from just a few fossils.

The shattered skull of a *Pachycephalosaurus* has been reassembled by comparing the fossilized fragments with similar dinosaurs. The fragments are held together with a paler filler.

DELVING DEEPER

Scientists can now see below the surface of fossil bones using X-rays, medical scanners, and a variety of other techniques. One of these involves analysing the annual "growth rings" in the bones of some dinosaurs. Here, the white arrows point to the rings in a *Tyrannosaurus rex* bone, which show how old the animal was when it died as well as how quickly it grew. Scanners can reveal things like brain size and shape, giving clues to a dinosaur's intelligence and sensory perception.

The crest of *Corythosaurus* is known from a fossilized skull, but we do not know what it looked like in life. It may have been brightly coloured and patterned.

The frill along the back of *Corythosaurus* is clear in fossil skin impressions, so we can guess that related dinosaurs had the same feature.

Newly discovered microscopic details of fossil feathers may even give evidence of colour.

BEYOND THE BONES

Studying and experimenting with the bones and teeth of a dinosaur can reveal how strong they would have been. We can test some of these ideas by building full-scale replicas like this *Tyrannosaurus* skull and jaw, which this experiment shows were strong enough to bite through the steel roof of a car!

SPECULATION AND THEORY

Although some facts about extinct dinosaurs are clear from the fossils, we have to guess at others. By comparing dinosaur remains with those of living animals and by using common sense, scientists can propose theories for discussion and further investigation. This never-ending study and debate is how science works.

Dinosaurs in action

For years people pictured dinosaurs as lumbering, half-witted giants, but new discoveries and scientific techniques are revealing a more exciting reality. We now believe them to have been agile, active creatures of very different sizes, and while they were not very intelligent, they may not have been quite so stupid as we once thought. In fact Mesozoic dinosaurs probably behaved more like athletic modern birds than overgrown lizards. And since birds are actually dinosaurs, the comparison makes a lot of sense!

Compsognathus was an agile, lightweight hunter that may have preyed on insects and other small animals.

LITTLE AND LARGE

For most of us, the word "dinosaur" conjures up an image of a colossal animal, possibly of terrifying ferocity. Some dinosaurs certainly were huge, and included the biggest creatures that have ever lived on land, while others, like the late Jurassic *Compsognathus,* were small, nimble creatures, more like chickens than anything else. Even many well-known dinosaurs were smaller than most people think; *Velociraptor* was just 1.8 m (6 ft) long.

WALKING TALL

Some early illustrations of giant dinosaurs showed them sprawling on the ground like lizards, and even being forced to live in water to buoy up their heavy bodies. But close study of the way their bones fit together shows that they supported their weight on legs that were upright beneath their bodies, and even the biggest sauropods probably held both their heads and tails well off the ground.

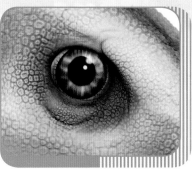

SHARP SENSES

Since both birds and crocodiles have excellent colour vision, it is likely that their Mesozoic dinosaur relatives did, too. Some dinosaurs had very large eyes and optic nerves, indicating sharp sight. Studies of their skulls show that many had a well-developed sense of smell as well as good hearing.

Long-necked sauropods such as *Barosaurus* held their heads high, even when moving from place to place, and reached up even further to feed in the treetops.

The giant sauropods were the biggest of the dinosaurs – earth-shaking titans that could weigh as much as 13 elephants. Only the gigantic blue whale can grow bigger.

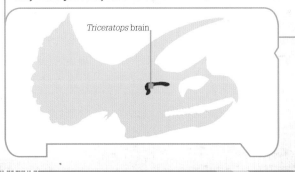

HIGH VELOCITY

Fossilized footprint trails have shown that some dinosaurs were super sprinters. Long-legged ostrich dinosaurs like *Gallimimus* could probably have matched modern ostriches in the running stakes; ostriches can keep up a steady 50 km/h (30 mph) – and even reach 70 km/h (43 mph)!

INTELLIGENCE

The brains of many dinosaurs such as *Triceratops* are very small compared to their body size, which suggests that these animals were not very intelligent. However, predatory dinosaurs had bigger brains, and for good reason: Successful hunting takes planning, aided by memory, which helps predators to exploit the habits of their prey. But although some theropod hunters were clever by dinosaur standards, they were probably no smarter than a chicken.

Triceratops brain

NEW LOOK

Many dinosaurs – mainly the bigger ones – had scaly reptilian skin, as you might expect. But recent fossil finds make it clear that some smaller dinosaurs, like this *Microraptor* from China, had long feathers, or were covered in slender "proto-feathers" that would have looked like hair. The feathers of some species could have been brightly coloured, just like the pretty plumage of many modern birds.

Supercharged

It is clear that many dinosaurs were agile, highly active animals, more like modern birds or mammals than typical, slow-moving, cold-blooded reptiles. This makes it likely that most dinosaurs were warm-blooded – generating their own body heat from food energy to supercharge their systems for a dynamic, fast-paced lifestyle.

CENTRAL HEATING

A cold-blooded reptile such as a crocodile relies on the sun to keep it warm and active. By contrast a bird or mammal – and probably a dinosaur – turns food into heat to keep its body at an ideal temperature, so that it can stay active even when the weather is very cold.

Fuzzy proto-feathers – slender filaments that would have acted like insulating fur – are clearly present on *Sinosauropteryx* fossils.

KEEPING WARM

Feathers provide excellent insulation for warm-blooded animals, enabling tiny songbirds to keep warm even in the coldest winters. The bodies of many small dinosaurs were covered with downy feathers, so they were probably warm-blooded, too.

Lesothosaurus and other small dinosaurs were built like gazelles, and must have had the same high-energy way of life.

Huge eyes probably helped *Leaellynasaura* to see in the dark.

CLIMATE EVIDENCE

By the early Cretaceous, continental drift had carried some regions close to the poles. Parts of what is now Australia lay at 75 degrees south, where it was dark for three months of the year and the winter climate was icy. Despite this, dinosaurs lived here. The best known is *Leaellynasaura* – a small ornithopod that may have sheltered in underground burrows. Since few cold-blooded animals can live in such cold climates, this dinosaur was almost certainly warm-blooded.

Adult *Apatosaurus*

Baby *Apatosaurus*

GROWTH RATE

Dinosaurs grew fast. Bone analysis shows that the mighty *Apatosaurus* – a 26-m (85-ft) colossus – grew at a rate of a few tonnes a year, from just a tiny hatchling to a 24-tonne adult. This is evidence that it was warm-blooded, because modern warm-blooded animals grow much faster than cold-blooded ones. If so, it means that gigantic sauropods such as *Apatosaurus* had the same warm-blooded physiology as their small, feathered counterparts.

The long-legged build of many dinosaurs such as *Camptosaurus* may have evolved so that they could range widely in search of the food they needed.

VITAL OXYGEN

Turning a lot of food into energy requires a lot of oxygen, and so efficient lungs are essential. Birds have very efficient lungs to provide the extra energy that they need for flight, and there is good evidence that they inherited these lungs from their Mesozoic ancestors.

FOOD AS FUEL

Roughly 80 per cent of the food eaten by a warm-blooded animal is turned into body heat, so it must eat five times as much food as a similar-sized cold-blooded animal, which gets its heat from the sun. This is one reason why plant-eating dinosaurs had massive guts for efficient digestion, and why later forms evolved super-efficient chewing teeth.

LIVE FAST, DIE YOUNG

Most modern reptiles lead long, slow lives. By contrast birds and mammals grow quickly, burn a lot of energy, and get a lot done in a short time. Evidence of rapid growth and short lives among dinosaurs suggests that they had the same high metabolic rate – they lived fast and died young.

Sphenosuchus was a small crocodilian, which also seems to have been far more agile than most modern reptiles.

Hunters & scavengers

For some reason, everyone's favourite dinosaur is one of the biggest killers that ever stalked the land – *Tyrannosaurus rex*. But Mesozoic hunters weren't all bone-crushing giants – many were small, agile animals that specialized in catching small prey, or picked at the remains of animals killed by other dinosaurs. Meanwhile, terrorizing pterosaurs might drop in from the sky, while ferociously predatory marine reptiles patrolled the oceans.

Tenontosaurus falls prey to a *Deinonychus* pack

Teeth and claws

Nearly all of the meat-eating dinosaurs of the Mesozoic era were theropods – saurischians that stood on their hind legs and, in general, had long necks, long tails, blade-like teeth, and sharp claws for seizing and killing their prey. They included the most powerful and notorious land predators of all time.

STEAK KNIVES
The teeth of a typical theropod were curved blades with very sharp serrated edges, like steak knives. They were ideal for butchering prey, but hunters like this *Allosaurus* also used them as weapons, slashing at the more vulnerable parts of their victims to inflict gaping, deadly wounds.

EARLY HUNTERS
The earliest true theropods found so far are the coelophysids, named after *Coelophysis* – a slender 3-m- (10-ft-) long hunter that lived in the late Triassic and early Jurassic. It is well known because hundreds of skeletons have been found, many at Ghost Ranch in New Mexico, USA. It had a long, flexible neck and quite long front limbs with strong fingers, and it stood on powerful hind legs that were balanced by a long tail. This basic body plan was typical of theropods, although some later types would depart from it quite radically.

The "sail" on this creature's back was up to 1.8 m (6 ft) tall and was probably for display.

More than 100 small, sharp, curved, serrated teeth could be found in the long, narrow jaws of *Coelophysis*.

A long, heavy tail balanced the enormous weight of the animal's head and upper body.

Each hand had three strong functional fingers for grasping prey, and a very short fourth finger.

Three toes supported the dinosaur's weight, but it had another small toe on the inside surface of its foot, near the back, as all theropods did.

Big "sickle claw" was usually held well clear of the ground to keep it sharp, but *Deinonychus* could sweep it down to deliver a killer blow.

SUPER SENSES

Hunters need acute senses to detect their prey and mount an attack. Many had good stereoscopic vision for 3-D perception and judging distance – vital for an accurate strike. *Troodon*, an agile late Cretaceous hunter of small animals, had very big eyes that were linked to unusually large optic lobes in its brain, as well as highly specialized ears that probably gave it very keen hearing. Other theropods, such as the tyrannosaurids, had large areas of the brain dedicated to a finely tuned sense of smell for sniffing out hidden prey.

KILLER CLAWS

Most theropods had strong forelimbs armed with sharp claws. One group in particular – the maniraptorans – had very well-developed arms and hands. Some maniraptorans such as *Deinonychus* and *Velociraptor* also had an upturned "sickle claw" on each foot that was almost certainly their main weapon.

SMALL AND AGILE

Many theropods were relatively small, nimble creatures. This fossil *Sinosauropteryx* from China is just 68 cm (27 in) long; it was a chicken-sized hunter that would have preyed mainly on insects, lizards, and small mammals, and was probably hunted in turn by bigger killers. The fine detail of the fossil shows that the animal was covered with short, dark, fur-like feathers to retain body heat.

The longest upper teeth fit into a notch in the lower jaw – just like the jaws of a crocodile.

BONE CRUSHERS

The most famous predatory dinosaurs are the tyrannosaurids – creatures such as *Tarbosaurus*, *Albertosaurus*, and, of course, *Tyrannosaurus rex*. But they were not typical theropods. Their forelimbs were tiny, while their strong jaws were armed with massive, deep-rooted teeth that could crush bone. We know this because their fossilized dung (below) is full of bone fragments!

FISHING GIANTS

Some theropods specialized in eating fish. They included the biggest so far discovered – the mighty *Spinosaurus*, which grew to a colossal 16 m (52 ft). Its jaws were like those of a modern crocodile with long, pointed, interlocking teeth that were ideal for gripping slippery, struggling fish. But it would have seized and eaten many other types of animals, too; one spinosaurid fossil revealed young *Iguanodon* remains in its stomach.

Strong, three-fingered hands armed with sharp claws were perfect for seizing fish.

Tyrannosaur attack

The true skin colour of *Tyrannosaurus rex* is unknown, but it is likely that its shape was disguised by a cryptic camouflage pattern. This would help it to get closer to its victims before mounting an attack.

CRIPPLING BITE

Typical hunting dinosaurs probably used their strongly clawed hands to grip their prey while they took slashing bites with their slender, blade-like teeth. By contrast, tyrannosaurs had much shorter arms but far stronger jaws, studded with bone-crunching teeth that were more like sharp spikes than blades. This enabled *Tyrannosaurus* to rush in and take a crippling bite without clinging to its struggling victim.

A tyrannosaur's feet were big and strong to support its weight. They were armed with stout claws that may have helped it to subdue struggling prey.

FAVOURED PREY

Tyrannosaurus rex lived at the end of the Cretaceous period in what is now North America. One of its main victims was *Edmontosaurus* – a big, duck-billed hadrosaur. We know this because *Edmontosaurus* skeletons have been discovered with tyrannosaur bite marks. In one instance the bite had partly healed, providing evidence that the tyrannosaur was a hunter of live animals and not just a scavenger of carcasses.

The most powerful land predator that ever lived, *Tyrannosaurus rex* was massively built with immensely strong jaws and teeth. These equipped it for a uniquely devastating attack technique – charging straight in and biting huge chunks out of its living victims.

AGILE STANCE

Outdated pictures of *Tyrannosaurus* show it sitting back resting on its tail. Today, scientists think that it stood with its body horizontal and its long tail held out stiffly to balance its heavy head, making it a highly agile hunter.

POWERFUL LEGS

1 The muscular legs have most of their bulk concentrated high up in the massive thighs and upper calves, so the lower limbs are quite slim. This type of leg form is typical of fast-running animals such as deer and horses – so, despite its huge weight, *Tyrannosaurus* was probably a fast mover.

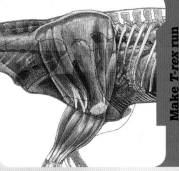

Make T-rex run

HUGE SKULL

2 The very deep, weighty skull and jaw were unusually strong and heavily muscled, giving *Tyrannosaurus* the colossal chomping power it needed to bite straight through bone. We don't know what this animal sounded like, but we can be fairly sure it was terrifyingly loud!

Make T-rex roar

The arms of *Tyrannosaurus* were quite strong – despite being tiny compared to the rest of its body – and each hand had two sharp-clawed fingers.

A big adult dinosaur would provide *Tyrannosaurus* with far more meat than it could eat all at once. It may have shared its prey, or defended it from others for several days.

Large, sensitive eyes gave *Tyrannosaurus* very sharp sight, like that of an eagle. They also faced forward, providing excellent 3-D vision for judging an attack.

The enormous, well-rooted teeth were strong enough to bite bones in half. If a tooth broke, it was soon replaced by a new one.

Egg-thieves and anteaters

We tend to picture all theropods as sharp-toothed meat-eaters, but they were far more diverse than this. Some had beaks rather than teeth, and many were adapted for eating insects, seeds, and plants rather than meat. Some small theropods took to the air as birds and still thrive today, 150 million years after their first appearance in the late Jurassic.

The unusually tall, crested, turkey-sized *Rinchenia* is known only from fossils found in Mongolia.

OSTRICH DINOSAURS

Closely related to – but very different from – the tyrannosaurs, ornithomimosaurs were slender omnivores with small, beaky heads. With the exception of their clawed hands, they looked just like ostriches, and one is even known as *Struthiomimus* – "ostrich mimic". Like modern ostriches they probably fed on leaves, fruit, twigs, seeds, and small animals, and were built for speed.

A toothless beak was a feature of all advanced ornithomimosaurs. More primitive types had very small teeth.

BEAKED HUNTERS

Some of the strangest theropods were the oviraptorids of the late Cretaceous – long-legged creatures with long feathered arms, short skulls, and often tall crests. Many had short beaks instead of teeth, but most had two bony projections from the roof of the mouth that would have been ideal for cracking eggshells; scientists therefore think they may have eaten eggs, as well as small animals and some plants.

Long, slim legs and slender feet would have helped *Struthiomimus* to speed away and escape its enemies, just like a gazelle.

SLOTH DINOSAURS

An even odder selection of creatures than the oviraptorids, the therizinosaurs, or sloth dinosaurs, of the Cretaceous period were maniraptoran theropods that seem to have given up hunting in favour of eating leaves. They had very long necks that allowed them to reach up into the trees, and small, leaf-shaped teeth. They also had very large guts, which would have been needed to digest a leafy diet.

Huge claws like scythe blades were a handy, deadly defensive weapon of the tyrannosaur-sized *Therizinosaurus*.

FEATHERED ANTEATERS

Alvarezsaurids, like the chicken-sized *Shuvuuia*, were feathered theropods with long, flexible necks, beaky jaws, and tiny teeth. They had unusually short arms with only one functional finger on each hand. But these arms were very strongly built for their size, and it is likely that these odd little dinosaurs used them to rip into the nests of ants and termites, making them the late Cretaceous equivalents of anteaters.

CLIMBERS AND GLIDERS

Many small, feathered theropods seem to have lived up in the trees, scrambling through the branches and even gliding between them. Animals like *Protarchaeopteryx* had feathered arms that may have helped them climb tree trunks – running vertically upwards while flapping their proto-wings to help their sharp-clawed feet to grip the bark.

AIRBORNE!

Taking the next step from gliding between branches, some maniraptoran theropods moved on to true powered flight. The pioneers were toothed dinosaurs with long, bony tails and small flight muscles, but over time they acquired shorter tails, stronger muscles, and sturdier, lighter skeletons for a better flight physique. By the early Cretaceous, high fliers such as these fossilized *Confuciusornis* were looking very like the birds that live all around us today.

Long hands and claws were probably used to gather food such as leaves, fern fronds, juicy shoots, and buds.

Soarers and stalkers

For most of the Mesozoic the skies were dominated by pterosaurs – close relatives of dinosaurs that appeared in the late Triassic and included some of the largest flying animals that have ever existed. Highly specialized for flight, they swooped down to prey on animals ranging from insects to young dinosaurs.

FLYING REPTILES

The earliest pterosaurs yet discovered were crow-sized, long-tailed reptiles like this *Rhamphorhynchus*. They were fully adapted for flight with bat-like wings that were formed from membranes of elastic skin. Each wing was supported by the bones of a single extended finger and powered by big pectoral muscles that were fuelled by a highly efficient respiratory system, much like that of birds and other saurischian dinosaurs.

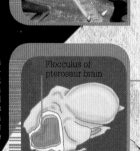

Most early pterosaurs had long snouts, typically with many sharp teeth. Some had several types of teeth, and the complex shapes of some of the teeth suggest that these animals chewed their food rather than swallowing it whole.

All pterosaurs had an unusually large flocculus – the part of the brain that monitors sensory input from the muscles, joints, skin, and balance organs. This indicates that the brain was constantly correcting the wing profile to improve its efficiency.

Flocculus of pterosaur brain

The bodies of all pterosaurs were covered with a kind of fur. This would have helped to keep them warm, indicating that these animals were almost certainly warm-blooded.

All early pterosaurs had long, bony tails. Some fossils show evidence of a small, fleshy vane at the tail tip that the animal would have used as a rudder to help steer it through the air. These long-tailed pterosaurs disappeared in the late Jurassic.

PTERODACTYLS

During the Jurassic, new types of pterosaur evolved – the pterodactyls. These had longer necks and much shorter tails than the earlier types. They also had longer wing bones and much longer, stronger legs. They had larger brains, possibly for improved flight control, and many of them had big, spectacular crests of bone and horn on their heads.

ALL FOURS

Many pterosaurs probably hunted on the wing. But the strong-legged pterodactyls were also well equipped for walking on all fours, by folding their wings up from the base of the "wing finger" and walking on the other fingers; fossil trackways preserve evidence of this. This *Pterodactylus* had big webbed feet, suggesting that it foraged on waterlogged mud. Others, such as the giant *Quetzalcoatlus,* had smaller feet that were better suited to dry, hard ground.

The hugely elongated fourth (ring) finger supported the wing's leading edge. The rest of the wing was stiffened by reinforcing fibres and muscles, which could alter the wing shape in the sky to make the pterosaur a more efficient flyer.

DIVERSE DIETS

Many of the early pterosaurs were probably insect-eaters. Others were well equipped for catching fish, with long, needle-like teeth for piercing slimy skin. Many pterodactyls had no teeth at all in their long, sharp-beaked snouts, and while some of these ate fish, others probably preyed on small dinosaurs. A few had stranger diets: *Pterodaustro*, shown here, had up to 1,000 bristle-like teeth in its long, upcurved lower jaw – ideal for filtering shallow water for small aquatic animals.

AIRBORNE GIANTS

During the Cretaceous, small pterosaurs became scarce and eventually disappeared, leaving just larger ones. The biggest of these were giant azhdarchids such as *Quetzalcoatlus* – an aircraft-sized animal that stood as tall as a giraffe and weighed at least 20 times as much as the heaviest flying birds today. But it was clearly well equipped for flight – perhaps more so than any animal before or since.

Oceanic hunters

The other main group of predators in the Mesozoic were the marine reptiles. With their sheer size and ferocity, huge jaws and teeth, they had a lot in common with the largest theropods, but were only distantly related to dinosaurs. Although they breathed air, most were highly adapted for aquatic life.

CRUNCHY DIETS

During the Triassic, shallow coastal seas were populated by a variety of chunky marine reptiles called placodonts. Some of the later types like these *Henodus* had stout shells like turtles, and probably fed on the sea bed. Their teeth were mainly big and flat – ideal for crushing thick-shelled molluscs and brachiopods. They also had strong teeth protruding from the fronts of their mouths, which they might have used to prise shellfish off rocks.

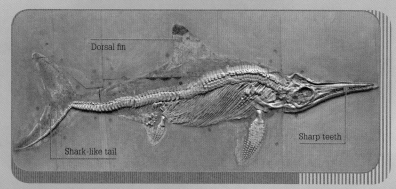

Dorsal fin

Shark-like tail

Sharp teeth

MESOZOIC DOLPHINS

Some of the best-known marine reptiles are the ichthyosaurs – sleek hunters with shark-like fins and tails that appeared in the early Triassic and persisted until the mid-Cretaceous. Many of the early ones were shellfish-eaters, but typical Jurassic ichthyosaurs like *Stenopterygius* ate fish and squid-like ammonites. A few preyed on other marine reptiles, including smaller ichthyosaurs.

The very long, pointed teeth of *Nothosaurus* were ideal for gripping slippery fish.

BEACH BREEDERS

Patrolling the shallow coastal waters of Triassic oceans were the nothosaurs. They had four legs with webbed feet or flippers, and although they hunted in the water they almost certainly bred on beaches and coastal rocks, much like seals do today, and gave birth to live young – unlike egg-laying dinosaurs. *Nothosaurus* itself had a long, flexible neck that allowed it to throw its head to one side and seize passing fish in its sharp teeth.

Each foot was webbed for swimming, but had five strongly clawed toes for walking on land as well.

SEA DRAGONS

As long ago as 1823 the fossil hunter Mary Anning found the first known skeleton of a "sea dragon", or plesiosaur. These animals were related to the nothosaurs, but were fully aquatic with four long flippers. Typical plesiosaurs had long necks and small heads, and their stomach contents show that they ate a lot of shellfish. They probably gathered these while swimming slowly over the sea bed. However, some types, such as *Elasmosaurus,* had long, sharp teeth that would have been useful for catching fish.

Wing-like flippers were used by plesiosaurs to drive themselves through the water.

Long teeth that protruded from the front of its jaw would have made *Elasmosaurus* an efficient fisher.

The incredibly long neck of *Elasmosaurus* had more than 70 vertebrae – more than any other known animal.

The jaws of the largest pliosaurs were up to 3 m (10 ft) long.

The colossal skull of *Kronosaurus* was nearly twice the size of a tyrannosaur skull.

TOP PREDATORS

There were two main varieties of plesiosaurs – the long-necked, small-headed ones and short-necked, big-headed pliosaurs such as *Kronosaurus*. These formidable foes were clearly dedicated hunters, with huge jaws armed with stout, sharp, crocodile-like teeth. They would have preyed on plesiosaurs and other marine reptiles, as well as large fish, and were the top predators of Mesozoic oceans.

Nothosaurs and their relatives – which included plesiosaurs and pliosaurs – had highly modified shoulder bones that made their front limbs better adapted for powerful swimming strokes.

MARINE LIZARDS

The early Cretaceous saw the appearance of the mosasaurs – relatives of modern monitor lizards that were adapted to marine life with paddle-like limbs. They swam with sinuous body movements like crocodiles, and were probably skulking ambush predators. Some were giants, such as this 15-m (49-ft) *Mosasaurus*, with the strength to attack and overpower other big marine reptiles such as long-necked plesiosaurs.

Shock tactics

The Mesozoic oceans were patrolled by the most powerful predators that ever lived on land or sea – giant pliosaurs. These real-life sea monsters were the marine equivalents of *Tyrannosaurus rex*, with the muscle and weaponry to kill and eat virtually anything they ran – or swam – into. Their only enemies were huge sharks – and each other.

A short tail, possibly with a low fin, was probably used by *Rhomaleosaurus* to steer as it drove itself through the water with its long flippers.

MASSIVE ATTACK

A murderously effective hunter of the Jurassic oceans, *Rhomaleosaurus* used its acute sense of smell and excellent eyesight to stalk its prey before charging into the attack with its massive jaws gaping wide, inflicting devastating wounds to cripple its victim. Then, if the prey was too big to swallow whole, *Rhomaleosaurus* would tear it apart to reduce it to manageable mouthfuls, gulping each piece down without chewing it.

Relatively short but very muscular neck was built for wrenching at strong, struggling prey.

Excellent vision would have enabled *Rhomaleosaurus* to target its victims with deadly accuracy during the final attack.

Sensory organs in the roof of the mouth detected any scent of prey in the water, so that it could track down its quarry from a distance like a shark.

PREY

It is likely that *Rhomaleosaurus* ate a lot of fish – especially big, meaty ones – but it would also have targeted other marine reptiles like this *Ichthyosaurus*, and even big, long-necked plesiosaurs. Some fossilized marine reptile bones show deep bite marks that were almost certainly inflicted by the sharp teeth of predatory pliosaurs such as *Rhomaleosaurus*.

The bones of the hands and feet were modified to form long, flat, pointed flippers. They were all the same shape, and *Rhomaleosaurus* probably used them to "fly" through the water rather like a modern sea lion, but using all four limbs instead of just two.

The fearsome and predatory *Rhomaleosaurus* was bigger and more powerful than the largest modern crocodile.

JAWS AND TEETH

1 The pointed teeth of a *Rhomaleosaurus* were just like this crocodile's – ideal for seizing prey and delivering killer bites. Its immensely strong skull suggests that it clamped its jaws tight and shook its victims apart, ripping and twisting just as crocodiles do today.

Pointed teeth

Make *Rhomaleosaurus* attack

Plant processors

A *Barosaurus* herd makes a meal of some conifer leaves

Hunting is difficult and dangerous. Life is much easier for an animal that can just eat the plants growing all around it. This was especially true during the Mesozoic when the plants of the era – such as horsetails, ferns, conifers, cycads, and ginkgos – were more nutritious than similar plants today. Yet plants are more difficult to digest than meat, so many plant-eating dinosaurs had special adaptations for the job. Others had to choose their food carefully…

Picking and choosing

Plant food is easy to find, but leaves in particular are not so easy to digest. Some dinosaurs evolved ways of processing them more efficiently, but others solved the problem by being more selective, looking for more easily digested tender shoots, juicy roots, fruits, and seeds. They supplemented these with worms, insects, eggs, and nestlings – meet the omnivores.

OMNIVOROUS ANCESTORS

Many early dinosaurs were omnivores, and it is likely that the ancestors of all dinosaurs – animals that resembled this late Triassic *Silesaurus* – were omnivores, too. Since an omnivore eats a variety of foods it is very adaptable, giving it an edge during periods of environmental change such as in the Triassic, when dinosaurs first appeared.

SIZE MATTERS

Most of the very early "plant-eating" ornithischians were quite small, so they could not devour large quantities of bulky leaves – they needed a more concentrated diet. The early Jurassic *Lesothosaurus* was typical of these dinosaurs – a turkey-sized, agile biped with simple, unspecialized teeth that probably ate insects as well as a variety of plant material.

Long legs and a lightweight frame helped to make *Lesothosaurus* a fast runner.

Big eyes would have given *Heterodontosaurus* good all-round vision for avoiding trouble.

DUAL-PURPOSE TEETH

The giant, plant-eating sauropods of the Jurassic evolved from smaller animals called prosauropods. These were mainly bipedal, with long-fingered hands rather than stumpy front feet. They had leaf-shaped chewing teeth and pointed front teeth, so they probably ate both plants and small animals – indeed, one prosauropod was found with the skull of a small reptile in its stomach.

Long, powerful hind legs supported the weight of the early Jurassic *Lufengosaurus*.

Mobile hands were better suited to gathering food than bearing the animal's weight.

Long, pointed teeth look just like those of a wolf, and some scientists think *Heterodontosaurus* was a full-time carnivore.

The skull of *Heterodontosaurus* shows the sharp contrast between its cheek teeth and long "canine" teeth. Having such different types of teeth – known as heterodonty, which accounts for the animal's name – is very unusual for a dinosaur.

DENTAL RIDDLE

Heterodontosaurus is one of the most puzzling dinosaurs of the early Jurassic. An early ornithischian with a sharp, horny beak like other ornithischians, it also had long, pointed "canine" teeth at the front of its mouth as well as closely packed chisel-shaped cheek teeth. While its beak would have been useful for gathering leaves, the pointed teeth look more suitable for seizing small prey. So it is likely that *Heterodontosaurus* ate both plants and animals.

Thick dome on top of the skull, which was ringed with a crown of spikes, gave pachycephalosaurs – meaning "thick-headed lizards" – their name.

The beaked *Pachycephalosaurus* had serrated, leaf-shaped teeth at the side of its mouth, nipping teeth at the front, and tall, conical teeth in its bottom jaw.

FRUIT AND NUTS

Flowering plants became common in the late Cretaceous, providing dinosaurs with new foods such as fruit and nuts. This encouraged the evolution of new types of omnivores such as the pachycephalosaurs – ornithischians with several types of teeth in their jaws. They probably ate a wide variety of foods, including fruit and small animals.

Powerful hind legs gave this dog-sized dinosaur the speed to catch small animals and escape from bigger ones.

Sturdy arms with long, grasping hands might have been used by *Heterodontosaurus* to dig up roots and grab small animals.

This oviraptorid had a beak and no teeth, but scientists are unsure about what it ate.

OMNIVOROUS THEROPODS

Typical theropods were hunters, but during the Cretaceous a number of odd theropods appeared that – judging from their teeth – seem to have eaten plant material as well as small animals. Some, such as oviraptorids and ostrich-like ornithomimosaurs, had beaks rather than teeth, and they may have behaved very like large, flightless birds.

Leaf-eating giants

The biggest and most spectacular dinosaurs were the long-necked sauropods. One reason for their size was that they needed big stomachs and long guts to digest large quantities of their leafy, low-value food. The larger they were, the more they could eat and the more nutrients they could extract. As a result, they were some of the biggest animals that have ever lived.

ALL FOURS

One of the first sauropods was *Isanosaurus*, a 6-m- (20-ft-) long animal that lived in the late Triassic. Unlike the earlier prosauropods it walked on all fours, which helped support a large digestive system. But it could probably rear up on its hind legs to reach high leaves, and had mobile front toes that it may have used to gather food.

Mamenchisaurus had 19 neck bones, and one specimen had a neck 13 m (43 ft) long! A typical dinosaur had 9 or 10 neck bones.

HIGH BROWSERS

One of the most distinctive features of a sauropod was its long neck. The neck of the late Jurassic *Mamenchisaurus* accounted for half of its total length! As with all sauropods, the neck bones contained cavities that were probably filled with respiratory air sacs, like those in theropods and modern birds. This made the bones lightweight and allowed the sauropod to raise its head high to feed in the treetops with relatively little effort.

The tail was almost as long as the neck and may have been used as a defensive weapon.

Long, heavy tail was held high off the ground.

The skull has big eye sockets but only room for a very small brain.

All the teeth of *Diplodocus* were right at the end of its snout – ideal for cropping leaves, but not for chewing them.

LEAF RAKERS

Most sauropods had relatively tiny heads and small jaws with simple, spoon-shaped teeth. But the late Jurassic *Diplodocus* and its relatives had peg-like teeth at the front of a broad snout, which it may have used like a rake to strip leaves from branches. Since it had no chewing teeth it swallowed the leaves whole, enabling it to eat a lot in a short time. The leaves were fermented in its enormous hindgut to release the nutrients.

The massively built back limbs were about 4.5 m (15 ft) long. Each hind foot was supported by a wedge-shaped pad of fatty tissue to spread the animal's immense weight.

The spine was reinforced with muscles and tendons that helped to hold up the animal's long neck and tail.

Typical sauropods had quite simple teeth. But rebbachisaurids such as the mid-Cretaceous *Nigersaurus* were quite different, with tiny teeth forming straight rows across the front of its squared-off snout. Each row was backed up by at least seven more rows, which moved forward to replace the active teeth as they wore out. They would have been ideal for grazing, but grass had not evolved at this stage of the Mesozoic, so *Nigersaurus* must have eaten some other tough, probably low-growing, vegetation.

The back legs were much stronger than the front ones, suggesting that *Isanosaurus* could rear up to eat leaves growing high in the trees.

The long neck was supported by special peg-and-socket joints between the bones that helped to keep the spine rigid.

The skull of *Argentinosaurus* has never been found, but it probably had all of its teeth concentrated at the front of its jaws, rather like *Diplodocus*.

HIGH AND MIGHTY

Although most sauropods looked rather similar, their body proportions varied. The colossal front legs of the late Jurassic *Giraffatitan*, for example, were longer than its back ones – reversing the usual arrangement. This gave it a very high reach when feeding in the treetops. However, the great weight of its forequarters probably stopped it from rearing up on its hind legs as other sauropods did, so it may not have been able to reach any higher, but at 26 m (85 ft) long and up to 18 m (59 ft) high, this probably didn't matter.

The gigantic body contained an enormous digestive system for extracting as much nutrition as possible from the animal's leafy, fibrous food.

Diplodocus   *Giraffatitan*

SHEER SIZE

The large sauropods were the biggest animals that have ever walked on dry land. One of the largest discovered so far is *Argentinosaurus* – a late Cretaceous titanosaur from Argentina. Its remains indicate that it was up to 36 m (118 ft) long and weighed as much as 13 elephants! Such creatures are far bigger than any other land animal that has ever existed, and scientists are debating whether there was something special about the Mesozoic environment that encouraged their evolution.

The largest sauropods were 10 times the size of *Tyrannosaurus rex*.

Beaked browsers

The ornithischians were a major and diverse group of dinosaurs, distinguished by an extra bone at the jaw tip that supported a beak. Like the sauropods they were mostly herbivores, but were generally much smaller. Even so, some were spectacular animals, especially the armoured thyreophorans – the first of the main ornithischian groups to appear.

All ornithischian dinosaurs had a special predentary bone – unique to this dinosaur group – at the tip of the lower jaw, covered by a beak.

Scutellosaurus had rows of small bony "scutes" embedded in its skin.

Leaf-shaped teeth were those of a plant-eater.

ARMOURED DINOSAURS

The first ornithischians were small dinosaurs that walked on their back legs. In the early Jurassic they gave rise to a group called the thyreophorans, or "shield bearers", because they were armoured with bony plates. *Scutellosaurus*, a lightly built biped, is the earliest of these armoured dinosaurs discovered so far.

WEIGHED DOWN

Over time, the thyreophorans became bigger and more heavily defended. As their armour became thicker and weightier, they started using their forefeet to help support their bodies. One of the first of these four-footed thyreophorans was *Scelidosaurus*. It probably fed on low-growing plants, since its short neck did not allow it to reach high into the trees and it was not built for rearing up on its hind legs.

HEAVY BRIGADE

In the early Jurassic, the thyreophorans split into the stegosaurs and the ankylosaurs. Stegosaurs like this *Stegosaurus* had rows of tall plates projecting from their backs, while the ankylosaurs had thick armour that was sometimes extended into long spikes. Many of these dinosaurs grew very big, and they all supported their considerable weight on all four legs.

Plates were not part of the skeleton

Defensive tail spikes

This massive animal walked on its toes.

Hips were a lot higher than the shoulders

The tiny brain of this rhinoceros-sized dinosaur would have weighed no more than a small apple.

Rows of tall, bony knobs extended down the neck, back, and tail of *Scelidosaurus*, forming an effective body armour.

Kentrosaurus had no teeth in the tip of its snout, but gathered its leafy food with the sharp edges of its horny beak.

BEAKS AND TEETH

Like all ornithischian dinosaurs, the thyreophorans had beaks at the tips of their jaws. A beak is useful for cropping vegetation, enabling these animals to be more selective than the giant, long-necked sauropods, and to gather tender, more digestible foliage. They sliced or chewed the leaves with their simple leaf-shaped cheek teeth to release some of their nutritious juices before swallowing them.

The front legs and feet of *Scelidosaurus* were adapted to bear its weight. All of the later thyreophorans shared the same four-footed build.

The barrel-shaped body of the ankylosaur *Euoplocephalus* had plenty of room to house a big digestive system.

BIG STOMACHS

Although not in the same league as the giant sauropods, stegosaurs and ankylosaurs had big, capacious stomachs and long intestines. This meant that they could swallow large quantities of leafy material and digest it for a long time to extract all of the nutrients. But unlike sauropods they sliced or chewed their food so that they could digest it more efficiently.

Food factories

Some time after the thyreophorans appeared, the other ornithischians divided into the ornithopods and the marginocephalians. Both groups included animals that were equipped with complex teeth for pulping tough plant material, releasing its nutritious juices and making it easier to digest. They were among the most numerous and successful of all dinosaurs.

AGILE LIGHTWEIGHTS

The earliest ornithopods were relatively small dinosaurs that ran on their long hind legs. They had beaks and simple leaf-shaped teeth, and were probably selective feeders that ate only the juiciest shoots. They included the early Cretaceous 2-m (6-ft) *Hypsilophodon* – one of the first small dinosaurs to be identified, in 1869.

The almost horse-like skull of *Iguanodon* had long jaws studded with leaf-shaped teeth that resemble those of a modern iguana – which accounts for its name.

Iguanodon had strong middle fingers to support its weight, but its long fifth finger could be bent over to gather food. Its first finger was modified into a stout, conical spike, which it probably used for fighting and in self-defence.

POWERFUL JAWS

The primitive ornithopods gave rise to the iguanodonts, named after the early Cretaceous *Iguanodon*. This 10-m (33-ft) herbivore had long, powerful jaws that were equipped with many chewing teeth – but, as with all iguanodonts, tipped with a completely toothless beak. It probably walked mainly on all fours, feeding on the ground and supporting its weight on its strong arms and multi-purpose hands, but could also rear up to reach for food high in the trees.

GRINDING TEETH

In the late Cretaceous, the iguanodonts were giving way to the duckbills, which had very long snouts tipped with broad, toothless beaks. The more advanced duckbills such as *Edmontosaurus* had multiple rows of teeth that formed a big grinding surface, with new teeth constantly moving in to replace worn ones. This enabled the duckbills to chew and digest their leafy food very efficiently.

The broad beak of *Edmontosaurus* was well adapted for gathering leafy foliage from bushes and trees.

The small stones lying in the stomach region of this superb *Psittacosaurus* fossil are almost certainly gastroliths, used to help grind its plant food to a pulp.

STOMACH STONES

Some birds swallow stones to grind up the food that they have eaten, retaining them in a muscular, tough-walled gizzard. These stones are called gastroliths. We once thought that giant sauropods used gastroliths, too, because they had no chewing teeth. This now seems unlikely, but some ornithischian dinosaurs, such as the early Cretaceous *Psittacosaurus*, must have used gastroliths because they have been found inside their remains.

PARROT BILLS

The marginocephalians included ceratopsians such as the late Cretaceous *Triceratops*, which is well known for its bony neck frill and long horns. Like the duckbills they had toothless beaks at the tips of their jaws, and multiple rows of cheek teeth. However, their teeth worked in a different way, shearing like scissor blades to slice their leafy food rather than grinding it up. The system must have worked well, because these animals were very successful.

The beaks of ceratopsians like this *Triceratops* were narrow and pointed like those of parrots.

Defence & display

The Mesozoic was an era of fearsomely powerful predators. Survival depended on being alert and fast, or having strong defences. As hunters became more formidable, so the defences became more elaborate, allowing them to be used as display features in rivalry disputes and to impress potential mates. Other dinosaurs were adorned with purely ornamental crests and feathery plumes, which may have been vividly coloured. It is now clear that many of these animals must have been truly spectacular.

A group of the impressively armed *Triceratops*

Plates and spikes

One defence against sharp-toothed predators is a thick hide reinforced with bony armour. The earliest armoured dinosaurs had small bony knobs in their skin, but by degrees these evolved into thicker plates that were often extended into spines. Some species also carried sharp spikes or heavy, bony clubs on their strong, mobile tails, enabling them to defend themselves more actively. And of course they could always bite back.

BONY DEFENCES

Many dinosaurs had bony structures called osteoderms embedded in the skin, which were covered with a thick layer of horn to form defensive plates. Early thyreophorans such as *Scutellosaurus* had several hundred osteoderms extending down the neck, back, and tail, and several Cretaceous titanosaurs (late sauropods) had them, too; notably *Saltasaurus*, which was studded with thick, flattened, roughly circular plates.

The armour of *Saltasaurus* extended from head to tail. It must have provided some protection from the sharp teeth of the massively built hunters of late Cretaceous Argentina.

PLATE ARMOUR

As predators got bigger, so the defences of their armoured prey became stronger. Some ankylosaurs acquired thick plates that were proof against most attackers, especially typical theropods with long, but quite slender, blade-like teeth that were likely to snap off on impact with a bony plate. But by the late Cretaceous, some predators – the tyrannosaurids – had much stouter teeth that could smash bone. This forced the evolution of giant armoured quadrupeds like *Ankylosaurus*, the ultimate "tank dinosaur".

TAIL SPIKES

Stegosaurs such as *Stegosaurus* are famous for their tall dorsal plates, but they also had sharp spikes projecting sideways from the tip of the tail. *Allosaurus* tail bones have been found with damage that must have been inflicted by *Stegosaurus* tail spikes – swept sideways, the spikes would have pierced the body of an attacker, inflicting substantial wounds that would have discouraged many predators.

Astonishingly long shoulder spikes and rows of armour plates on its back made *Sauropelta* virtually impregnable to attack.

The tail spikes of *Stegosaurus* pointed up in early reconstructions of the dinosaur, but scientists now think that they faced sideways, making a much more effective weapon.

SHARP SPINES

Plates can easily develop into stout spines as animals evolve, and these were to become a feature of a group of ankylosaurs known as nodosaurids. Some of these, such as the early Cretaceous *Sauropelta*, had spectacularly long spines on their shoulders. These must have been at least partly for show, but they would have impressed enemies as well as rivals – an effective deterrent to hungry predators.

The beak of *Protoceratops* was clamped around its enemy's arm, as in this reconstruction, but the animals died together when they were both buried by a collapsing sand dune.

LEG-BREAKER

Many dinosaurs used their tails for defence. Heavily muscled, yet containing no vital organs, they made ideal weapons. The tails of nodosaurids like *Sauropelta* were fringed with sharp plates to maximize their impact. Those of the related ankylosaurids were tipped with a solid club, which, swung in the right direction, must have been capable of breaking the leg of a tyrannosaur.

BITE BACK

One other group of dinosaurs – the ceratopsians – developed what looks like serious armour and weaponry. They included the well-known *Triceratops*, with its bony neck shield and long horns. But it is likely that these animals relied more heavily on their powerful parrot-like beaks, which they could use to bite attackers and inflict deadly injuries. A famous fossil found in Mongolia in 1971 shows a *Protoceratops* fighting off a *Velociraptor* in just this way. The predator's claws were embedded in the *Protoceratops*, but its arm was trapped in the beak and was almost certainly about to be bitten right off.

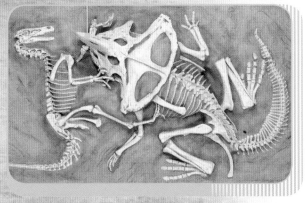

Fighting back

The armoured dinosaurs evolved their bony defences for protection, but over time some also acquired weapons for fighting back. The most devastating of these were the hefty tail clubs of the big ankylosaurs, which were probably heavy enough to kill some predators outright.

Rows of ridged, oval, bony plates extended down the animal's back. These plates would have been covered with tough horn, and some supported tall spikes.

The head was covered with interlocking bony plates that may have been attached directly to the skull, forming a very tough armour.

Euoplocephalus's short, deep snout with a horny beak housed complex structures inside the nasal cavity that may have enhanced its sense of smell.

Make a predator attack

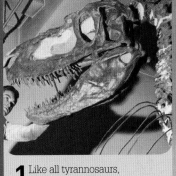

POWER BITE

1 Like all tyrannosaurs, *Gorgosaurus* had a heavily built skull and jaw and an immensely powerful bite. If it could get close enough to *Euoplocephalus* it might have been able to smash through its armour – fossil evidence shows that this sometimes happened. But first it had to evade that bone-breaking tail club.

TOP PREDATOR

Although *Gorgosaurus* was much lighter than its monstrous relative *Tyrannosaurus* – which lived some six million years later – it was still a massive animal. It would have been the top predator of its time in what is now western North America, with no serious enemies. But a single misjudged attack on an animal like *Euoplocephalus* could leave it crippled, and it might die of its injuries or slowly starve to death.

The tail bones supporting the club were fused together into a rigid rod, like a hammer handle. Most movement was from the base of the tail.

The spike-shaped teeth were strong enough to bite through bone without snapping, so *Gorgosaurus* was a serious threat even to an armoured ankylosaur.

HEAVY WEAPON

The massively built, rhino-sized *Euoplocephalus* was one of several big, club-tailed ankylosaurs that appeared in the late Cretaceous. Their weapons would have been lethally effective against smaller predators, but they probably evolved as a defence against their most fearsome enemies – the huge, heavily armed tyrannosaurs. Slammed into the leg of an attacking *Gorgosaurus*, the heavy tail club could easily inflict a crippling injury.

Euoplocephalus even had armour plates covering its eyelids.

The short, thick, pillar-like front legs had hoof-like toes and very thick bones to support the ankylosaur's weight on all fours.

TAIL CLUB

2 The tail club was formed of four bony plates that were fused together to form a sledgehammer-like solid lump. It was swung from side to side, and all that weight on the end of the animal's long tail ensured a shattering impact. But the club was quite strong enough to withstand this, even if the enemy's bones were not.

Make Euoplocephalus defend itself

Avoiding trouble

The best survival strategy for any animal is to stay out of trouble, and dinosaurs were no exception. The biggest ones may have trusted in their size to deter attackers, but small ones had to be more careful. If they could hide, they would. Otherwise they could run away, and many small dinosaurs were clearly built for speed. Failing that, they could stick together for mutual security. There is evidence that many dinosaurs lived in groups and even big herds, probably for this reason.

The turkey-sized *Othnielosaurus* was typical of many small, agile ornithischian dinosaurs that relied on their speed to escape danger.

An ancient burrow found in Montana, USA, contained the fossil remains of the small plant-eater *Oryctodromeus* and its young. *Oryctodromeus* was well adapted for digging, so it probably burrowed underground to nest as well as to escape danger.

LYING LOW

Many dinosaurs were no bigger than small kangaroos or wild turkeys, so they could easily hide among the lush Mesozoic vegetation. This would conceal them from enemies that hunted by sight, but not from those that tracked their prey by scent – and some theropods had an excellent sense of smell. We now know that some small ornithopods dug burrows, so these may have bolted underground like rabbits when danger threatened. But was this common among small dinosaurs? We don't know.

Dark backs and pale bellies were probably common in many dinosaurs, reducing the shadow effect beneath the body and making it less easy to see.

CAMOUFLAGE

While some predatory dinosaurs were able to sniff out their prey, others relied more heavily on their eyes, so it is likely that many small dinosaurs were well camouflaged to blend into the background. As long as they kept still, they might avoid being seen. Some may have had cryptic patterns to disguise their shape, while others were just drably coloured. But many may have given up the advantages of camouflage in favour of vivid display colours, just like many modern birds.

QUICK GETAWAY

One thing we definitely know is that many dinosaurs were quick on their feet. Small ornithischians like *Othnielosaurus* were built like gazelles, with long, slender legs and powerful muscles. These animals were basically plant-eaters, so they didn't need to be fast to catch prey. Instead, they used their speed to avoid being caught and eaten by other dinosaurs. In turn, the predators – even giants like *Tyrannosaurus* – developed similar adaptations for speed so that they could chase down their fast-running quarry.

IMPREGNABLE GIANTS

You might think that an adult giant sauropod would be too much for most hunters to take on, but they were not impregnable; a fossilized trackway in Texas shows the footprints of a colossal brachiosaurid being chased by a predatory *Acrocanthosaurus*. The tracks come together at one point, and it is likely that the hunter grabbed hold of the big sauropod in an attempt to bring it down. So it is clear that giants like this *Supersaurus* were attacked by hunters such as *Allosaurus*, even if few such assaults were successful.

BACK-UP

There is plenty of trackway evidence for plant-eating dinosaurs travelling together in compact groups. This has several advantages, including more eyes to watch for danger, and less chance of being picked off during an attack because a predator will normally take only one victim. Some dinosaurs may have even joined forces to drive off enemies in a counter-attack. But they had to keep together, because so many prey animals would be a huge temptation to predators, and any stragglers would have made easy targets.

The thick undergrowth and dappled shade of Mesozoic forests would have encouraged the evolution of camouflage.

Dressed to thrill

Some dinosaurs had features that, at first sight, look as if they were for defence against predators. But many were far too elaborate and flimsy for this purpose, and it is more likely that they were for show. The animals probably used them in displays that were designed to intimidate rivals, raise their social status, and impress potential mates.

The spikes on the tail were definitely defensive; we know this from fossils that show the wounds they inflicted on predators such as *Allosaurus*.

SHOWING OFF

Some antelope and deer have very long or elaborate horns or antlers. These species are always social animals that use their weapons in contests for social status and mates. Sometimes, simply parading an impressive set of headgear is enough to ensure victory – but sometimes it isn't, and animals clash in ritual combat, like these red deer stags. Deer are very different from dinosaurs, but it is thought that many dinosaurs may have behaved in the same way.

The bony extension of *Chasmosaurus*'s skull would have supported an impressive but lightweight frill.

HORNS AND FRILLS

Many of the late Cretaceous ceratopsians have extravagant frills and horns on their heads. In some cases, such as *Chasmosaurus*, the long, bony frill on the back of the skull is perforated with large holes to reduce its weight. This would have made it useless as defensive armour, so it must have evolved as a display feature to impress other animals of the same species.

Dramatically long spikes protruded from the neck and shoulders of *Edmontonia*.

PLATES AND SPIKES

The plates and spikes of late Cretaceous ankylosaurs were definitely defensive, but some seem more flamboyant than was necessary. They were probably dual-purpose features – providing defence against enemies such as tyrannosaurs, but also used to impress rivals and possibly spar with them.

HIGH PROFILE

The huge dorsal plates of *Stegosaurus* and its relatives have always been a mystery. They can have had very little defensive value, since they do not protect its body. According to one theory they functioned as heat exchangers for warming up or cooling down, but the horn-covered bony plates would not have contained enough blood vessels for this. It is far more likely that the plates were display features, dramatically enhancing the animal's appearance.

Each plate was up to 60 cm (24 in) high, with a bony core covered by skin and tough, probably colourful, horn.

DOMES AND CROWNS

Pachycephalosaurs such as *Stygimoloch* are known as boneheads because of their hugely thickened skulls, which formed high domes that were often fringed with crowns of spikes. They may have used these for head-butting in rivalry contests, but some experts think that this would have put too much strain on the head or neck, and that they were purely for display.

SPINY SAUROPODS

Most sauropods were not flamboyant creatures, but there were some exceptions. The neck of the early Cretaceous *Amargasaurus* sprouted a double row of long, bony spines, which could have been covered in horn or may have supported two webs of skin. Either way it would have been an impressive display feature. Others such as *Agustinia* – a titanosaur – had both spines and plate armour.

The skin was probably distinctively coloured to make *Stegosaurus* easily recognizable by others of the same species, as it is thought that dinosaurs had good colour vision.

The spines protruding from the neck of *Amargasaurus* were extensions of the neck vertebrae. Some were more than 1 m (3 ft) long.

MALES AND FEMALES

Modern animals with spectacular display features are usually males. Does this mean that the most flamboyant dinosaurs were all males, too? If so, where are the females? Possible male and female forms of *Protoceratops* have been identified, but there are also intermediate forms, so maybe both sexes had the same adornments and *Protoceratops* was just very variable. There is no evidence of distinct male and female forms of other dinosaurs.

Male *Protoceratops*...?

Female *Protoceratops*...?

The curled crest of *Cryolophosaurus* ran across the head just above the animal's eyes. Its bony core probably had a sheath of horn.

CRESTED HUNTERS

Some theropods had crests on their heads. These crests were generally quite small, but others were more impressive. The small tyrannosaur *Guanlong* had a large crest running the length of its snout, and an early Jurassic theropod found on Antarctica – which was much warmer in the Mesozoic era – had a bony quiff that earned it the nickname "Elvisaurus" before it was officially named *Cryolophosaurus*.

The dramatic crest of *Parasaurolophus* doubled the length of its skull, and its sound may have been as impressive as its size.

BONY TRUMPETS

Several duck-billed hadrosaurs had impressive bony crests that may have supported even more elaborate structures of skin and horny keratin – a strengthening skin protein. *Parasaurolophus* had a long extension from the back of its skull, containing a complex system of tubes that were linked to its nasal passages. The animal may have used this like a trumpet, to add resonance and volume to its calls. There are several species, and each has a different crest – so their calls probably sounded different, too.

Crests and plumes

Many dinosaurs had impressive crests on their heads or backs. These were almost certainly for display, either to rivals of the same sex or to potential mates. Others had feathers and some had very long, flamboyant plumes that could have been brightly coloured for the same display reasons. It seems likely that some dinosaurs were as colourful and spectacular as many modern birds.

The sail on the back of *Irritator* was almost certainly for show, making the animal's body look even bigger.

SOFT TISSUE

The bony crests preserved on many dinosaur skulls could have supported bigger structures made of soft tissue. The Cretaceous ornithopod *Muttaburrasaurus*, for example, may have had inflatable nasal sacs that amplified its calls in much the same way as the oversized nose of a bull elephant seal.

SAILBACKS

A few dinosaurs had extra-long spines projecting upwards from their vertebrae, which seem to have supported webs of skin and other soft tissue to form a "sail". They included the spinosaurids – big predators with crocodile-like jaws that fed mainly on fish. The sail of the biggest, *Spinosaurus*, was up to 1.8 m (6 ft) high, creating a dramatic display feature, and relatives such as *Irritator* were probably adorned in the same way.

The very long tail plumes of *Epidexipteryx* were surely ornamental.

PLUMES AND FANS

Fossils of small theropod dinosaurs found in China are so finely detailed that they have preserved their feathers as well as their bones. The fossils show complex vaned feathers on their arms, hands, tails, and sometimes legs. Since these animals were not equipped for flight, the longer feathers must have been at least partly decorative, and may have been vividly coloured.

FEATHERED GLORY

New research that employs electron microscope technology reveals that some fossil feathers preserve the remains of melanosomes – the structures inside cells that contain colour pigments. This technique has been applied to the 155-million-year-old fossils of *Anchiornis* – a chicken-sized theropod found in China – with exciting results. For the very first time, we have proof that at least one Mesozoic dinosaur had colourful, eye-catching plumage.

The striking red crown of *Anchiornis* is known from comparing the microscopic detail of its fossil feathers with those of modern birds.

The elaborate and colourful plumes of *Anchiornis* were probably very like those of related maniraptoran theropods such as *Velociraptor*.

Air show

Some of the most magnificent display ornaments were the crests of pterosaurs, especially the winged giants of the Cretaceous period. Some of the crests were so extravagant that it is hard to imagine how the animals flew efficiently, but they must have made a dramatic spectacle as they soared overhead.

The crest was held aloft by thin rods of bone at front and back, but was mostly made of horny keratin, like the coloured bills and feathers of birds.

A toothless beak was common to many of the big Cretaceous pterosaurs, and *Tupandactylus* was no exception. We don't know what it ate, but it probably preyed on insects and other small animals.

The incredible crest of *Tupandactylus* is the largest of any pterosaur yet known.

DIVERSE CRESTS

The pterosaurs are renowned for their elaborate headgear. *Tupandactylus* may have had the most impressive crest, but there were plenty of contenders to vie for the crown. Some, such as *Caulkicephalus*, had crests on their snouts as well as their heads. Others were just plain weird, such as *Nyctosaurus*, which had a bizarre, bony crest extending high above its head rather like an oversized deer antler.

Nyctosaurus   *Tupuxuara*   *Dsungaripterus*   *Caulkicephalus*

The wing membrane had a sheet of thin muscle sandwiched between layers of blood vessels and stiff yet pliable reinforcing fibres. The muscle constantly adjusted the wing profile to ensure it worked as efficiently as possible, all the time.

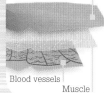

Reinforcing fibres

Blood vessels

Muscle

IMPERIAL CREST

Although it was definitely not the biggest pterosaur, *Tupandactylus imperator* was surely one of the most majestic. Its 79-cm (31-in) skull was crowned by long bony struts that supported an enormous crest resembling a giant fan or sail. The crest probably glowed with vivid colour, especially when the sunlight shone through its thin, translucent structure. It may have had some aerodynamic function, but was almost certainly mainly for show.

Each wing was supported at the front by long arm bones and a hugely elongated fourth finger. At the back they were probably attached to the legs.

GROUNDED

1 The huge, sail-like crest of *Tupandactylus* must have made flying quite difficult, especially on windy days. But, like all big pterosaurs, this animal was well equipped for walking on all fours with its outer wings folded up – it is likely that it didn't fly very much, except to travel from one feeding ground to another.

Make *Tupandactylus* land and walk

The feet of this animal have not survived as fossils, but they were probably quite small and well adapted for walking on firm ground.

Dinosaur society

Ever since the discovery
of nesting colonies in the 1970s,
we've known that some dinosaurs
lived in large groups for at least part of
the year, and the display features of many
species suggest that they would compete
for mates and possibly social status within
these groups. Later discoveries of footprint
trails known as trackways also indicate that
some travelled together, possibly in herds,
while analysis of the fossils from breeding
colonies hints towards a nurturing side
in some dinosaurs, protecting and
feeding their young.

A *Pachyrhinosaurus*
herd hits the road

Living together

Judging by the evidence of fossilized footprints and breeding colonies, dinosaurs had a social side. They probably lived together in one region all year, but some may have migrated from place to place, often travelling together in herds. It is also possible that some carnivores hunted in packs.

MAKING TRACKS

Fossilized footprint trackways show us that some dinosaurs were in the habit of walking together. One of the most famous trackways, in Colorado, USA, shows these big, circular footprints left by several big sauropods walking in a group. Other trackways were made by ornithopods and oviraptorids, and some show dozens of animals moving together, probably as a social group.

BONE BEDS

Some fossil sites preserve vast numbers of dinosaur remains in spectacular bone beds. In some cases these are all of the same species, such as those containing the hadrosaur *Edmontosaurus* and the ceratopsian *Centrosaurus*, both from late Cretaceous North America. In both cases, the animals seem to have been killed together by a local catastrophe such as a flash flood, so it is likely that they lived together, too. The remains of hundreds of animals of the same species suggest that they lived in big herds.

Albertosaurus was a smaller, lighter relative of *Tyrannosaurus* that lived in late Cretaceous North America.

HERDS AND COLONIES

Many modern animals that live in large groups are nomadic plant-eaters that work their way across the landscape, eating what they can. They live in a herd, often led by a few high-status individuals. This would make sense of the "status symbol" display features of dinosaurs like these *Parasaurolophus*, and the fact that these animals seem to have communicated by sound. Smaller social animals such as rabbits live in static colonies, but while we now know that some small dinosaurs did burrow, dino-warrens seem unlikely.

The arms of these hunters were probably too small to be used to grab hold of prey.

If some dinosaurs did live in big herds, it is possible that they made mass migrations from one feeding site to another, like these wildebeest on the African plains. The huge dinosaur herds suggested by the evidence of bone beds might have had to move on regularly to avoid destroying their food supply. In fact, some of these bone beds may mark river crossings and similar places where the migration route was especially dangerous.

TERRITORIAL PAIRS

Although some herbivores probably lived in nomadic herds, it is likely that most carnivores were territorial – claiming a patch of land as their own home range. Living in the same area year-round would allow them to learn the terrain and exploit its resources, just like foxes and owls do today. Territory holders like these tyrannosaurs would drive out rivals of the same species – with the exception of potential breeding partners.

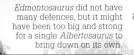

Edmontosaurus did not have many defences, but it might have been too big and strong for a single *Albertosaurus* to bring down on its own.

HUNTING TOGETHER

There are tantalizing clues that some predators hunted in family groups. On one site the remains of several *Deinonychus* were found with *Tenontosaurus* – a big plant-eater – and it's possible that the lightweight hunters had joined forces to attack it. A group of nine *Albertosaurus* has also been found in Canada, where they would have hunted the big hadrosaur *Edmontosaurus*. But they were not smart enough to use complex tactics, and probably just relied on brute force.

Long legs gave *Albertosaurus* the speed to catch its quarry, but it might need help to kill it.

Breeding colonies

One thing we definitely know about dinosaur society is that some dinosaurs nested in breeding colonies. Several have been found; some are very big and were apparently used for many years, like traditional seabird nesting sites. The females laid large clutches of eggs, and while some dinosaurs seem to have covered their eggs with plant material, like crocodiles, others used their body heat to incubate them like birds.

DINOSAUR EGGS

Plenty of fossilized dinosaur eggs have survived, showing that they were rather like modern birds' eggs, with hard, brittle shells. Some were smooth, others bumpy; many probably once had colours and patterns. Their shapes ranged from perfect spheres to elongated ovals. But the surprising thing is their size: Compared to the hen's egg seen here they were huge, but compared to an adult dinosaur they were remarkably small, indicating that dinosaurs grew very fast.

IDENTIFICATION

Eggs are rarely found associated with a parent dinosaur, so identifying them can be a problem. Scientists often end up giving them special names, known as "oospecies", which do not link them to known dinosaurs. But some eggs have survived complete with identifiable embryos inside. The most well-known are those of the small theropod *Troodon*, found intact in the egg because it was killed, by whatever buried the nest, before it hatched. Eggs with *Saltasaurus* and *Citipati* embryos have been found, too.

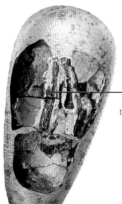

The fossilized bones of the tiny *Troodon* embryos, still in the eggs, were discovered in Montana, USA, in the 1980s. They were the first dinosaur embryos to be found.

This restoration of a *Troodon* embryo shows how the tiny dinosaur was curled up inside its oval egg with its long head tucked between its legs. *Troodon* was a small theropod that lived in the late Cretaceous.

MOUND NESTS

All dinosaurs seem to have laid their eggs in bowl-shaped ground nests. The most common nest form is a raised mound that was probably covered with vegetation. Each nest contained a lot of eggs. Hundreds of fossilized nests excavated in India in 2009 contained roughly eight eggs each, and *Maiasaura* nests found in Montana in the 1970s had up to 20. Even if only a few young survived, it meant that dinosaurs could multiply far more quickly than big mammals such as elephants.

These oviraptorid eggs found in the Mongolian desert have been laid in a roughly spiral pattern. This was typical of many nesting dinosaurs.

COLONIES AND PAIRS

A big breakthrough in dinosaur science was the discovery of breeding colonies of the hadrosaur *Maiasaura* in Montana in the 1970s. The nests were less than an adult's length apart, so they nested as closely as they could without annoying their neighbours. Some colonies were huge: a titanosaur nesting ground found in Patagonia in the late 1990s contained thousands of eggs. But other dinosaurs nested as isolated pairs, each within their own territory, just as many birds do today.

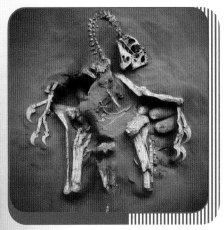

INCUBATION

Most dinosaur nests were covered with vegetation. As this decayed it generated heat that incubated the eggs. Crocodiles use the same system. But some smaller dinosaurs incubated their eggs using body heat, like chickens. In this fossil of the oviraptorid *Citipati*, two eggs are visible beneath one of its front limbs, which had long feathers to cover the eggs and keep them warm.

Deinonychus and other small theropods may have stolen a lot of their prey from dinosaur nesting colonies in the breeding season.

EGG-THIEVES

Some dinosaurs would have been egg-thieves, just like modern crows. This would have been a powerful motive for nesting in a colony, because the adults could jointly defend their eggs and hatchlings from raiders. Obviously these colonies would attract predators on the look-out for an easy meal, and the remains of several intruders have been found on dinosaur breeding sites among the nests and eggs.

Breaking out

We have fossil proof that some lightweight theropod dinosaurs incubated their eggs much like modern hens, covering them with their feathered arms to keep them warm. When the young hatched they were quite well developed, and able to leave the nest fairly soon to find food. But their parents may well have helped them, and even caught food for them to eat.

The body of *Citipati* was almost certainly covered with slender "proto-feathers" that looked like hair, and would have kept it warm.

SITTING TIGHT
Scientists working in the Gobi Desert of Mongolia have found at least four specimens of the long-armed oviraptorid *Citipati* with clutches of eggs. Each was sitting in the centre of its nest, surrounded by up to 20 eggs that it was sheltering beneath its feathered arms. The dinosaurs were surely incubating them using their own body heat, just like most modern birds. But they were hit by some disaster, such as a sandstorm, that buried and killed them.

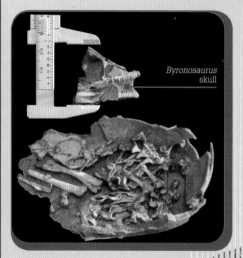

Byronosaurus skull

FOSSIL EMBRYO

The nest was a hollowed-out earth mound. Unlike some dinosaurs, *Citipati* did not nest in colonies.

In 1993, a *Citipati* egg was found complete with the skeleton of an unhatched baby – although it was not identified for several years. Nearby were the tiny skulls of two baby *Byronosaurus* theropods, each only 32 mm (1.25 in) across. It is possible that these were prey of the brooding parent.

The horny crest of *Citipati* formed part of its beak, like that of many other oviraptorids. The crest probably glowed with vivid display colours.

Although this animal had no true teeth, it had two bony knobs projecting from the roof of its mouth. It may have used these to crack eggs stolen from the nests of other dinosaurs.

Each *Citipati* egg was 18 cm (7 in) long – the size of a big mango.

Each arm had long feathers, rather like the flight feathers of a bird. These were partly for show, but also to cover the eggs in the nest and incubate them. *Citipati* may have brooded its hatchlings, too, in the same way.

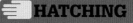

HATCHING

1 When the baby *Citipati* was ready to hatch, it would have used its beak to crack the tough shell. It is possible that its mother would have heard it squeaking in the egg and helped it break out to take its first breath of air. After all that hard work to release itself into the world, it would have rested for a few hours.

Make an egg hatch

UP AND ABOUT

2 Fossils of some baby theropods show that they had well-developed legs when they hatched. This suggests that *Citipati* would have been able to walk and leave the nest within hours of hatching. It might have chased insects, or picked at prey caught by an adult for its first meal.

Make the hatchling walk around the nest

The eggs of this dinosaur were elongated ovals, with tough shells rather like those of ostrich eggs. It is possible that the eggs in each nest were laid by more than one female and incubated by the male.

Raising a family

Since the discovery of dinosaur breeding colonies in the 1970s, we have learned a lot about dinosaur nesting habits and parental care. And as more fossils of common species are found, we are also starting to see how they changed as they matured and grew older. Slowly, we are building up a picture of dinosaur family life.

PROTECTIVE PARENTS

Just as some small dinosaurs incubated their eggs using body heat, some may have used the same method to keep their hatched young warm and protected. Unfortunately this didn't save the family of 34 *Psittacosaurus* babies, who were being sheltered by an adult when they were buried by a volcanic ashfall in early Cretaceous China.

HUNGRY NESTLINGS

Some of the *Maiasaura* nests found in Montana, USA, in the 1970s contained the remains of nestlings. The way their teeth were worn indicates that the parents brought them food, and their size range shows that they stayed in the nest until they had grown to at least a metre (3 ft) long, which would have taken several weeks. At first they may have been almost helpless, but they probably developed quite fast.

ACTIVE CHICKS

By contrast with *Maiasaura*, some hatchling theropods such as *Troodon* seem to have left the nest straight away. They may have followed their parents like this oystercatcher chick, feeding themselves but relying on the adults for protection. Or they may have foraged without adults, forming groups of young dinosaurs that were able to look after themselves.

Psittacosaurus was a primitive ceratopsian, completely unrelated to the theropods that are known to have incubated their young. This shows that many different types of dinosaurs were dedicated parents.

STICKING TOGETHER

We know that young dinosaurs often stuck together after leaving the nest, because the remains of several groups of young have been found. It seems likely that these were families that fed together, and were all killed at the same time by some local catastrophe. Sometimes the young are with adults, sometimes not. But there is trackway evidence that young dinosaurs travelled with adults, as in this *Pachyrhinosaurus* herd.

Display features changed shape with maturity.

The 34 babies were probably from a single family – this is quite possible considering that a modern alligator lays up to 50 eggs. The ability to breed fast was one secret of the dinosaurs' success.

The family would have been killed instantly by the hot volcanic ash.

CHANGING SHAPE

Most dinosaurs seem to have become mature quite young. This was often marked by a change in appearance. The remains of a *Pachyrhinosaurus* herd found in Alberta show that the immature dinosaurs had short brow horns and long nose horns, but when each animal reached maturity its long nose horn was transformed into a knobbly lump.

YOUTH AND AGE

Most dinosaurs died before they were 30 years old. They bred at an early age, had a lot of babies – thanks to large clutches of eggs – and died young. However, some large sauropods survived longer. Lucky ones reached the age of 50 or so, getting bigger every year. The rare remains of these giants, such as the huge leg bones, show that they were the biggest animals that ever walked on dry land.

Alvarezsaurid
A small, short-armed, possibly ant-eating Cretaceous theropod.

Ammonite
A marine mollusc with a coiled shell and octopus-like tentacles that was common in the Mesozoic.

Amphibian
An animal such as a frog that starts life in water, but turns into an air-breathing adult that can live on land.

Ankylosaur
One of the main types of ornithischian dinosaur, with an armoured body.

Ankylosaurid
A type of ankylosaur with a tail club.

Archosaur
One reptile group that includes the crocodilians, pterosaurs, and dinosaurs.

Azhdarchid
A giant Cretaceous pterosaur.

Biped
An animal that walks on two legs.

Bird
A type of maniraptoran theropod dinosaur.

Bone bed
A massive deposit of fossil bones.

Brachiopod
An extinct marine animal resembling a clam.

Brachiosaurid
A sauropod with long front legs, related to *Brachiosaurus*.

Breeding colony
A large group of animals that has gathered to breed in one place.

Browse
To feed on leaves gathered from trees or bushes.

Camouflage
A disguise that helps an animal to blend in with its surroundings.

Carnivore
Any animal that specializes in eating meat.

Ceratopsian
A horned dinosaur with a large neck frill, such as *Triceratops*.

Cold-blooded
Refers to a type of animal that relies on the temperature of its surroundings to warm up its body.

Conifer
A plant – usually a tall tree such as a pine – that carries its seeds in scaly cones.

Continental drift
The gradual movement of continents around the globe over millions of years.

Coprolite
A fossilized animal dropping, which often contains fragments of the animal's food.

Cretaceous
The third period of the Mesozoic, which began 145 million years ago and ended 65 million years ago.

Crocodilians
Crocodiles, alligators, and fossil relatives.

Cycad
A plant that bears its seeds in large cones, but has a crown of foliage like a palm.

Digestion
The breakdown of food into simpler substances that can be absorbed and used by an animal's body.

Dinosaur
One of a group of reptiles that supported their weight off the ground and were probably warm-blooded.

Display
In animals, a demonstration of fitness or strength, usually designed to impress a rival or mate.

Dorsal
On an animal's back.

Duckbill
See hadrosaur.

Electron microscope
An extremely high-powered electronic microscope.

Embryo
An unhatched or unborn baby.

Extinct
Having died out completely. An extinct species has gone for good.

Ferment
A process in which food is broken down into simpler substances without involving air.

Filaments
Thin, hair-like structures.

Fossil
The remains or traces of a living thing that survive decay or destruction, and are often turned to stone.

Gastroliths
Stones swallowed by some animals to help grind up food in the gizzard.

Ginkgo
One of a group of non-flowering plants that grows into a tree with triangular leaves.

Gizzard
A thick-walled part of the digestive system of some animals, in which food is mashed up by muscular action.

Hadrosaur
An advanced type of ornithopod dinosaur with a duck-like bill and batteries of chewing teeth.

Hatchlings
Baby animals that have just hatched from eggs.

Heat exchanger
A structure that absorbs or loses heat.

Herbivore
An animal that eats leafy plant material.

Horsetail
A primitive plant that produces spores, not seeds, and has thread-like leaves that grow from the stem in rings.

Ichthyosaur
One of a group of dolphin-like marine reptiles that was very common in the early Mesozoic era.

Iguanodont
An ornithopod dinosaur with a toothless beak at the front of its jaws, but chewing teeth at the back.

Impregnable
Immune to attack.

Incubate
To keep eggs warm so that they develop and hatch.

Insulation
In animals, anything that helps conserve body heat, such as fur or feathers.

Invertebrate
An animal without a vertebral column (backbone).

Jurassic
The second period of the Mesozoic era, which began 199 million years ago and ended 145 million years ago.

Keratin
A tough structural protein in hair, feathers, scales, claws, and horns.

Mammal
One of a group of warm-blooded vertebrates that feed their young on milk.

Maniraptoran
Literally "hand-grabber" – a type of theropod with powerful arms and claws.

Marginocephalian
A group of ornithischians that consisted of the horned dinosaurs (ceratopsians) and boneheads (pachycephalosaurs).

Mate
A breeding partner.

Mature
Old enough to breed.

Membrane
A thin, flexible sheet of a material such as skin.

Mesozoic
Literally "middle animal life" – the era of time that includes the age of dinosaurs. It began 251 million years ago and ended 65 million years ago.

Metabolic rate
The rate at which the body burns energy.

Migration
The regular, often yearly return journey that an animal makes in search of feeding areas or breeding sites.

Minerals
Natural chemicals found in rocks and soil.

Molluscs
Shellfish such as mussels and clams, plus snails and non-shelled relatives such as slugs and squid.

Nodosaurid
One of a family of ankylosaurs that did not have a heavy club on the end of its tail.

Nomadic
Refers to animals that wander from place to place.

Omnivore
An animal that has a broad but selective diet of both animal and plant material.

Optic lobes
Part of the brain that processes visual data.

Optic nerve
A nerve bundle linking the eyes to the brain.

Organism
A living thing.

Ornithischian
A member of the group Ornithischia, one of the two primary types of dinosaurs.

Ornithomimosaur
A bird-like theropod dinosaur, resembling an ostrich.

Ornithopod
One of the three main groups of ornithischian dinosaurs.

Osteoderm
A tough, often protective plate embedded in the skin, with a bony base and a covering of scaly keratin.

Oviraptorid
A theropod dinosaur with a beak and feathered arms, named after *Oviraptor*.

Pachycephalosaur
A type of ornithischian dinosaur with a very thick skull, including *Pachycephalosaurus*.

Pectoral muscle
Chest muscle, enlarged into flight muscle in pterosaurs and birds.

Physiology
The mechanical, physical, and chemical functions of a living thing.

Plesiosaur
One of a group of typically long-necked marine reptiles with four roughly equal-sized flippers that lived throughout the Mesozoic era.

Pliosaur
A highly predatory type of plesiosaur with a short neck, and large head and jaws.

Predator
An animal that hunts and kills other animals for food.

Predentary bone
A bone at the tip of the lower jaw of ornithischian dinosaurs.

Prey
An animal that is killed and eaten by another animal.

Prosauropod
An early, mainly plant-eating saurischian dinosaur, ancestral to the giant long-necked sauropods.

Proto-feathers
Hair-like structures evolved by dinosaurs for insulation, which later evolved into feathers.

Pterodactyl
An advanced type of pterosaur with a short tail, named after *Pterodactylus*. (*Also* pterodactyloid)

Pterosaur
A flying reptile with bat-like wings, each supported by the bones of a single very elongated finger.

Quadruped
An animal that walks on four feet.

Quarry
A prey animal targeted by a hunter.

Reptile
A vertebrate animal belonging to the class Reptilia. Typical reptiles are cold-blooded, but the class also includes warm-blooded pterosaurs and dinosaurs.

Respiratory system
The system used by an animal to obtain vital oxygen.

Saurischian
A member of the group Saurischia, one of the two primary types of dinosaurs. (*See also* ornithischian)

Sauropod
One of a group of big, long-necked, four-footed, plant-eating saurischian dinosaurs that appeared in the late Triassic and survived until the end of the Mesozoic era.

Scavenger
An animal that lives on the remains of dead animals and other scraps.

Scute
See osteoderm.

Spinosaurid
A large theropod dinosaur that had crocodile-like jaws for eating fish, named after *Spinosaurus*.

Stegosaur
An ornithischian dinosaur with rows of plates and/or spines on its back, named after *Stegosaurus*.

Stereoscopic
Seeing a scene or object with both eyes. This enables an animal to see in 3-D.

Tendons
Strong, slightly elastic, cord-like structures that attach muscles to bones.

Theropod
One of the two main groups of saurischian dinosaurs, which were mainly two-footed meat-eaters.

Thyreophoran
One of the three main groups of ornithischian dinosaurs, which included the stegosaurs and ankylosaurs.

Titanosaur
A type of sauropod dinosaur that evolved late in the Mesozoic era.

Trackway
A trail of fossilized dinosaur footprints.

Triassic
The first period of the Mesozoic, which began 251 million years ago and ended 199 million years ago.

Tyrannosaur
A term often used for a tyrannosaurid.

Tyrannosaurid
A short-armed theropod closely related to the powerful *Tyrannosaurus*.

Vertebrae
The bones that make up the backbone of an animal such as a dinosaur.

Warm-blooded
Refers to an animal that uses food energy to keep its body constantly warm, regardless of the temperature of its surroundings.

Index

Credits

Dorling Kindersley would like to thank Katie Knutton for additional artworks, Charlotte Webb for proofreading, and Jackie Brind for the index.

The publisher would like to thank the following for their kind permission to reproduce their photographs: (**Key:** a-above; b-below/bottom; c-centre; l-left; r-right; t-top)

4 Corbis: Nick Rains (tr/Background). **Getty Images:** (tc). **5 Corbis:** Inspirestock (tc/Background). **Getty Images:** Darrell Gulin (tr); Siri Stafford (tl/Background). **6-7 Getty Images. 8 Getty Images:** Last Refuge (tr); Elisabeth Pollaert Smith (crb). **Plate Tectonic and Paleogeographic Maps by C. R. Scotese, © 2007, PALEOMAP Project (www.scotese.com) :** (cla) (bl) (c). **9 Corbis:** Frans Lanting (clb). **Dorling Kindersley:** Natural History Museum, London (crb). **10 Dorling Kindersley:** Robert L. Braun - modelmaker (crb/Stegosaurus); Jon Hughes (cb/Sauropods). **10-11 Dorling Kindersley:** National Science Museum, Japan. **11 Getty Images:** Ethan Miller (ca). **12 Dorling Kindersley:** Natural History Museum, London (bl). **Getty Images:** AFP (tr); David Silverman (cl). **13 Dorling Kindersley:** Natural History Museum, London (cra). **Getty Images:** AFP (crb); David Silverman (clb). **14 Dorling Kindersley:** State Museum of Nature, Stuttgart (bc). **Getty Images:** Louie Psihoyos / Science Faction Jewels (bl). **14-15 Getty Images:** AFP. **15 BBC Photo Library:** (bc). **Dorling Kindersley:** Natural History Museum, London (tr). **Gregory M. Erickson, Ph. D.:** (cr). **17 Getty Images:** (clb). **18 Corbis:** Roy Botterell (cb). **Getty Images:** Tim Graham Photo Library (cra). **Two Guys Fossils:** (cl). **18-19 Corbis:** Paul A. Souders (br/Background). **20-21 Corbis:** Nick Rains (Background). **22 Dorling Kindersley:** Staatliches Museum fur Naturkunde Stuttgart (tr). **23 Corbis:** Simon Mossman / EPA (br). **Dorling Kindersley:** Peabody Museum of Natural History, Yale University. All rights reserved. (tl). **Getty Images:** O. Louis Mazzatenta (cra). **25 Corbis:** (bc); Louie Psihoyos (ca). **Photolibrary:** Oxford Scientific (OSF) (cra). **26-27 Getty Images:** Jason Edwards (Background). **27 Getty Images:** O. Louis Mazzatenta (cr). **The Natural History Museum, London:** Anness Publishing (ca). **Luis Rey:** (tc). **28-29 Dorling Kindersley:** Senckenberg Nature Museum, Frankfurt. **29 Nobumichi Tamura:** (cr). **Dr. Mark Witton:** (tr). **30 Getty Images:** De Agostini (tr). **30-31 Dorling Kindersley:** David Peart (Background). **31 Dinocasts.com :** Robert DePalma (bl). **33 Corbis:** Nature's Planet Museum / Amanaimages (br). **34-35 Getty Images:** Siri Stafford (Background). **36 Dorling Kindersley:** Carnegie Museum of Natural History, Pittsburgh (br). **Nobumichi Tamura:** (tr). **36-37 Corbis:** Radius Images (bc/Ferns); Kevin Schafer (Background). **37 Corbis:** Louie Psihoyos (br). **38-39 Getty Images:** Martin Ruegner (Bakcground). **39 Getty Images:** Ira Block (tr). **40-41 Getty Images:** Oliver Strewe (Background). **42 Dorling Kindersley:** Senckenberg Nature Museum, Frankfurt (c). **42-43 Novapix:** Raul Lunia (bl/Background). **44-45 Corbis:** Inspirestock (Background). **46 Photoshot:** Andrea & Antonella Ferrari (clb/Sky). **46-47 Corbis:** Alan Traeger (Background). **47 Black Hills Institute of Geological Research:** (bl). **48-49 Corbis:** John Carnemolla (Back ground). **49 Corbis:** Bettmann (tl). **50 The Natural History Museum, London:** Andrey Atuchin (c). **50-51 Corbis:** Radius Images (bc/Ferns); Kevin Schafer (Background). **51 Luis Rey:** (tc). **Science Photo Library:** Jaime Chirinos (cl). **52 Ardea:** Stefan Meyers (ca). **52-53 Getty Images:** Peter Hendrie (Background). **53 Bailey Archive, Denver Museum of Nature & Science:** (tr). **Dorling Kindersley:** The American Museum of Natural (br/Skulls). **Getty Images:** National Geographic (cr). **Luis Rey:** (br/Artwork). **54 Getty Images:** (Background). **55 Julius T. Csotonyi :** (br). **Luis Rey:** (tr). **Professor Fucheng Zhang:** (cr). **56 Luis Rey:** (bl). **57 Dr. Mark Witton:** (br). **58-59 Getty Images:** Darrell Gulin (Background). **60 Corbis:** Louie Psihoyos / Science Faction (tr). **Photolibrary:** age fotostock (bl/Background). **Science Photo Library:** Jim Amos (cl). **60-61 Alamy Images:** Jaak Nilson (Background). **61 Corbis:** Nigel Pavitt / JAI (tc). **Getty Images:** Jochen Schlenker (tr/Background). **62 Corbis:** Louie Psihoyos / Science Faction (c). **Museum of the Rockies:** (bc). **62-63 Corbis:** Louie Psihoyos. **63 Corbis:** Louie Psihoyos (cr). **The Natural History Museum, London:** John Sibbick (tc). **64 Corbis:** Louie Psihoyos (cl). **64-65 Corbis:** J.A. Kraulis / All Canada Photos (Background). **66 naturepl.com:** Bernard Castelein (bl). **66-67 Rex Features:** Jinyuan Liu. **67 Getty Images:** Darrell Gulin (tr); Louie Psihoyos (br). **Science Photo Library:** Laurie O'Keefe (cr)

Jacket images: Front: **Getty Images**: Digital Vision / Steven Errico cb; Photographer's Choice / Thomas Collins bc. Back: **Getty Images**: Photographer's Choice / Thomas Collins cl; **iStockphoto.com**: Mischa Gossen c

All other images © Dorling Kindersley
For further information see: **www.dkimages.com**